THIS BOOK BELONGS TO

____

Written and illustrated by Myha Le
First Edition

Published by ByMyha, LLC, California, www.bymyhale.com

ISBN: 978-1-971229-00-3 (eBook)
ISBN: 978-1-971229-01-0 (Paperback)
ISBN: 978-1-971229-02-7(Hardcover)

Printed in the United States of America

ETHAN EARNS HIS ROCKET SHIP

Dedicated to all children learning to dream big, work hard, and turn their ideas into something special.

By Myha Le

Ethan pressed his nose against the
toy store window.
On the top shelf stood the most
amazing thing he had ever seen.

A shiny red rocket ship.

"Mom! Look!"
Ethan squealed.
"It is shiny.
It has a pointy nose.
It is the best rocket ship
in the whole world!"
He pointed with one hand.
"Can I have it?"

Mom smiled. “It is a wonderful rocket ship, sweetie. But toys from the store cost money.” Ethan looked up at her. “Then let’s buy it.”
Mom gave his hand a gentle squeeze. “We need money to buy things. And money is something we earn.”

Back home, Ethan looked at his piggy bank. It was empty. Not one coin clinked inside.

Ethan plopped onto his bed with a sigh. Maybe he would find a lucky coin on the sidewalk. Maybe a money tree would grow in the backyard!

Mom sat beside Ethan and
tucked him into bed.
“What if you earned the money
yourself?” she asked.

Ethan blinked and sat up in bed.
"Me?" he said.
"Can kids earn money too?"

Mom nodded.
"Yes. When you help people with
jobs they need done,
like washing a car or walking a dog,
you can earn money."
Ethan sat up a little taller.
"I can help," he said.

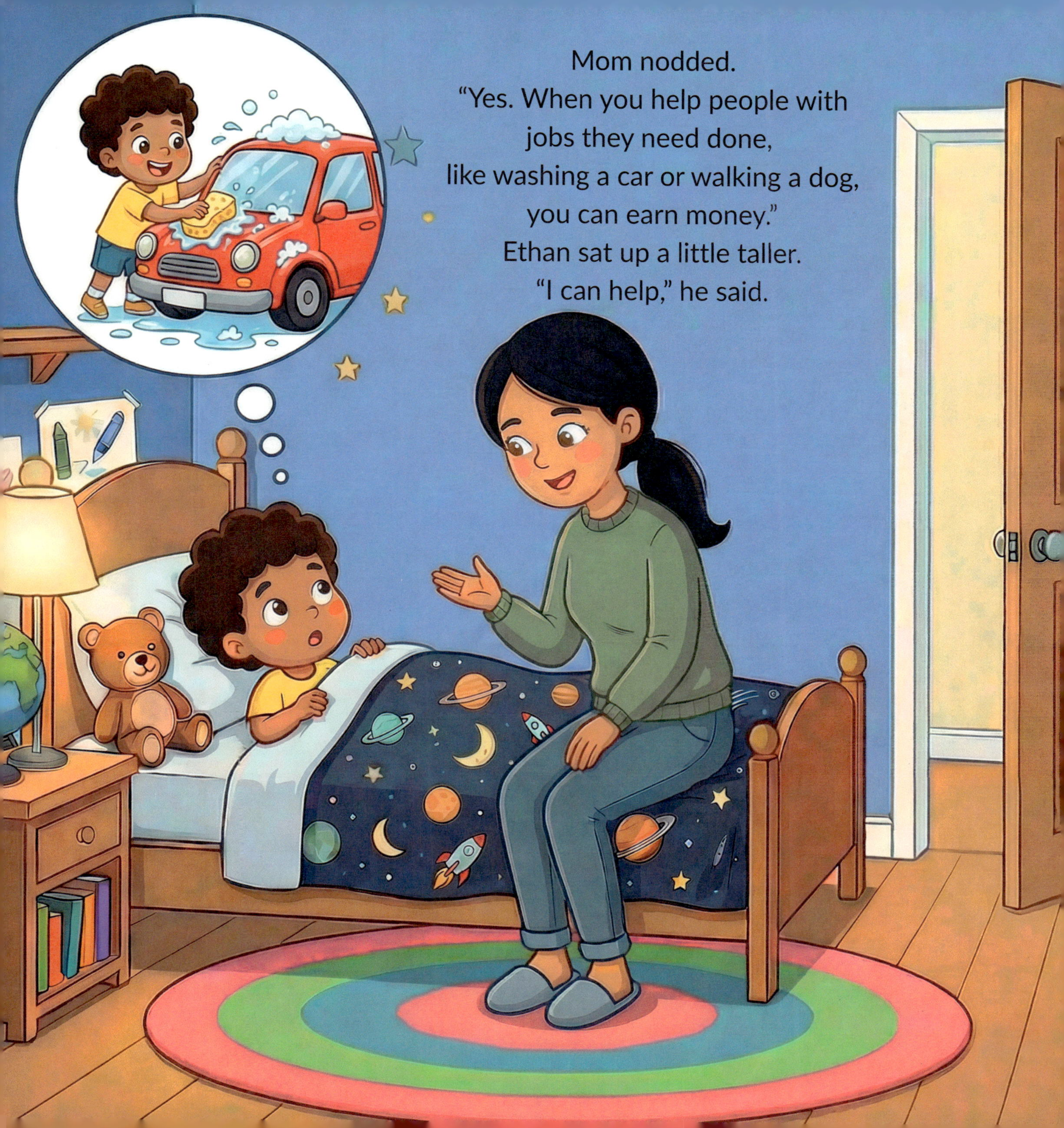

The next morning, Ethan grabbed his crayons and made a sign in big letters:

ETHAN THE SUPER HELPER

Then he smiled and said, "I am going to earn my rocket ship!"

First, Ethan helped Mom wash her car. He wiped the windows, scrubbed the doors, and made the shiny wheels sparkle in the sun.

Mom smiled proudly.
“Thank you, Ethan. You worked hard.”
She placed a shiny coin into his hand.

Ethan ran to his room
and dropped the coin
into his piggy bank.

CLINK!
Ethan smiled.
That was the best
sound yet.

Next, Ethan helped Mrs. Lopez walk her little brown dog. The dog wagged its tail, sniffed every flower, and trotted happily beside him.

"You were such a big help," said Mrs. Lopez.
She gave Ethan one shiny coin.

Across the street, Mr. Chen was getting ready to mow the lawn. "I can help," Ethan said. Mr. Chen pushed the mower, and Ethan helped by raking the fresh cut grass into neat little piles.

When the yard looked neat and tidy, Mr. Chen smiled. "Great job, Ethan. You worked very hard." He dropped a coin into Ethan's hand.

Then Ethan went next door to help
Mrs. Gable water her plants.
He gave the roses a long drink,
the daisies a splash, and the tiny
sprouts just enough.

"Oh, thank you, Ethan," said Mrs. Gable.
"You are such a thoughtful helper."
She gave him another shiny coin.

That evening, Ethan and Mom poured
all the coins onto the rug.
They counted together.
“One... two... three... four...”

Ethan leaned in close.
He was almost there. So very close.
"Just a little more," Mom said with a smile.

The next day, Ethan looked around the neighborhood for one more way to help. Then he spotted Mrs. Rivera carrying a grocery bag. “I can help,” Ethan said. He carried the bag all the way to her front door. She gave him one coin for his help.

Back at home, Ethan counted his money one more time. His fingers touched each coin, one by one. Then he looked up at Mom, and his whole face lit up. "I did it," he whispered. "I earned my rocket ship."

"You did," Mom said.
Ethan twirled around the room.
"I earned my rocket ship!
I earned my rocket ship!"

The next day, Ethan and Mom went to the toy store. Ethan held his little bag of coins tightly in both hands the whole way there.

At the counter, Ethan counted
out every coin all by himself.
The cashier smiled.
"I earned it," Ethan said proudly.
"I really earned it."

And then, at last, the shiny red rocket
ship was his. Ethan hugged it
close all the way home.
It felt big in his arms. And even
bigger in his heart.

Back in his room, the
rocket ship zoomed
through the air.

"Whooooosh!"

Past the bed.
Past the books.
Past the lamp.
All the way to the
moon and stars
in Ethan's imagination.

Ethan looked
at his hands.
These were the hands that
washed Mom’s car, walked
a dog, raked the grass into
little piles, watered plants,
and helped a neighbor
carry groceries.

Earning his rocket ship
made Ethan feel proud.

It was something he worked for.
Something he waited for.
Something he earned by
helping others.

And that made it the most
special rocket ship of all.

A NOTE FOR PARENTS AND GROWN UPS

Thank you for reading ***Ethan Earns His Rocket Ship***.

This story is about much more than buying a toy. It is about helping others, working toward a goal, and feeling proud of something earned through effort and patience.

Young children do not need big money lessons all at once. They learn best through simple conversations and everyday moments. Ethan's story gives you a gentle way to begin. After reading, you can ask:

- What did Ethan want most?
- Why could he not buy it right away?
- How did Ethan earn money?
- Which job would you want to help with?
- How did Ethan feel when he heard the first **CLINK** in his piggy bank?
- Why did the rocket ship feel more special after he earned it?

You can also help your child make the lesson real. Let them choose a small goal, think of simple ways to help at home, and count their coins as they save. These small steps teach children that money is connected to effort, choices, patience, and pride.

The conversations you start today can help build strong money habits for life.

KEEP THE MONEY CONVERSATION GOING

By visiting www.bymyhale.com

To discover more books, free coloring pages, and fun activity sheets designed to help children learn about money in a simple and meaningful way.

On our website, you will find stories and free printables that help families talk about:

- earning
- saving
- spending wisely
- helping others
- working toward a goal

Thank you for being part of the @bymyhale community.

THANK YOU FOR READING

If you and your child enjoyed *Ethan Earns His Rocket Ship*, please consider leaving a review on Amazon.

Your review helps other families discover books that teach children about money, hard work, patience, and helping others.

Thank you for supporting By Myha Le and for helping us bring financial literacy to more children, one story at a time.

Reviews mean so much to independent authors.

Thank you for your support.

-Myha Le, Author

Made in the USA
Monee, IL
05 November 2026

67381717R00021